PlayTime® P

Jazz & Blues

2011 EDITION

Level 1
5-Finger Melodies

This book belongs to: _____

Arranged by

Nancy and Randall Faber

Production Coordinator: Jon Ophoff
Cover: Terpstra Design, San Francisco
Engraving: Dovetree Productions, Inc.

FABER
PIANO ADVENTURES®
3042 Creek Drive
Ann Arbor, Michigan 48108

A NOTE TO TEACHERS

PlayTime® Piano Jazz & Blues is a fun collection of beginning jazz and blues pieces. The book offers a pleasing variety of sounds—from soulful blues to jazz originals and standards—and is a wonderful supplement for the late Level 1 piano student. The student will enjoy creating the sounds of jazz and blues while improving reading and rhythmic skills.

PlayTime® Jazz & Blues is part of the *PlayTime® Piano* series. "PlayTime" designates Level 1 of the *PreTime®* to *BigTime®* piano library arranged by Faber and Faber.

Following are the levels of the supplementary library, which lead from *PreTime®* to *BigTime®*.

PreTime® Piano	(Primer Level)
PlayTime® Piano	(Level 1)
ShowTime® Piano	(Level 2A)
ChordTime® Piano	(Level 2B)
FunTime® Piano	(Level 3A – 3B)
BigTime® Piano	(Level 4)

Each level offers books in a variety of styles, making it possible for the teacher to offer stimulating material for every student. For a complimentary detailed listing, e-mail faber@pianoadventures.com or write us at the mailing address below.

Visit **www.PianoAdventures.com**.

Helpful Hints:

1. Optional teacher duets are a valuable part of the *PlayTime® Piano* series, and these provide rhythmic vitality and harmonic interest.

2. While the duets can be used to inspire the student, the student should know his or her part well before playing with the duets.

3. Rehearsal numbers are provided to give the teacher and student starting places.

4. The teacher may wish to count a measure aloud before beginning.

About Jazz & Blues

Jazz and blues are distinctively American styles of music, characterized by improvisation and syncopated rhythm. Blues—an ancestor of jazz—can be traced back to the days of slavery, when American blacks began to combine African melodies and rhythms with Western harmony.

At the turn of the century, ragtime's syncopated rhythm took the country by storm—in fact Scott Joplin's piano rags were best sellers in his day. As blues and ragtime styles influenced each other, a dynamic swing style emerged which eventually became known as jazz. Championed in New Orleans by Jelly Roll Morton and Louis Armstrong, the new sound soared in popularity. By the 1920s, jazz had entered the mainstream of American popular music.

During the Swing Era of the 1930s and 40s, people were dancing to the big band sounds of Glenn Miller and other band leaders. The cool sounds of bebop followed in the 1950s, a time when solo artists such as Miles Davis and Charlie Parker infused jazz with a new seriousness—and ever since then jazz has continued to grow and change. Today the influence of blues and jazz can be heard in almost all popular music.

ISBN 978-1-61677-044-0

TABLE OF CONTENTS

Jeepers Creepers

Words by
JOHNNY MERCER

Music by
HARRY WARREN

Bright swing

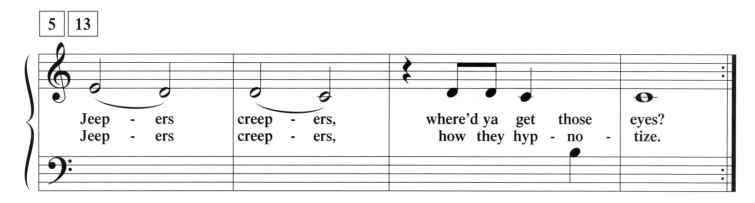

Teacher Duet: (Student plays 1 octave higher)

I'm Always Chasing Rainbows

Words by
JOSEPH McCARTHY

Music by
HARRY CARROL

Teacher Duet: (Student plays 1 octave higher)

Five Foot Two, Eyes of Blue
(Has Anybody Seen My Girl?)

Words by
JOE YOUNG and SAM LEWIS

Music by
RAY HENDERSON

FF1044

The Way You Look Tonight

Words by
DOROTHY FIELDS

Music by
JEROME KERN

FF1044

It's Only a Paper Moon

Lyric by
BILLY ROSE and
E.Y. "YIP" HARBURG

Music by
HAROLD ARLEN

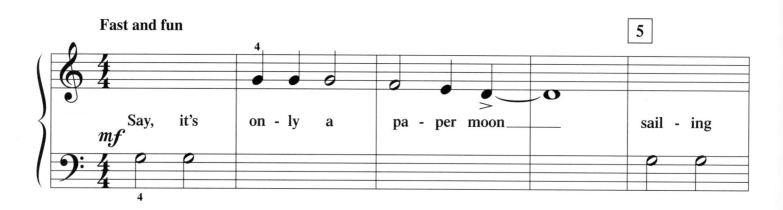

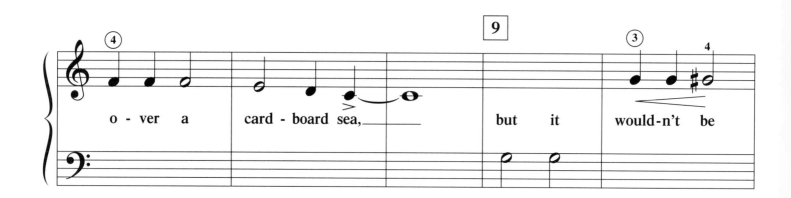

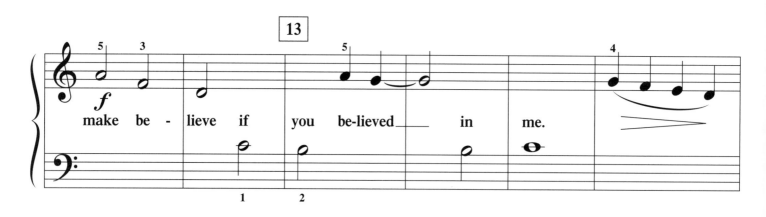

Teacher Duet: (Student plays 1 octave higher)

Yes, it's on-ly a can-vas sky hang - ing

mf

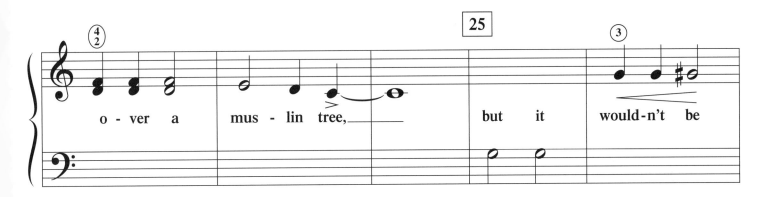

o - ver a mus - lin tree, but it would-n't be

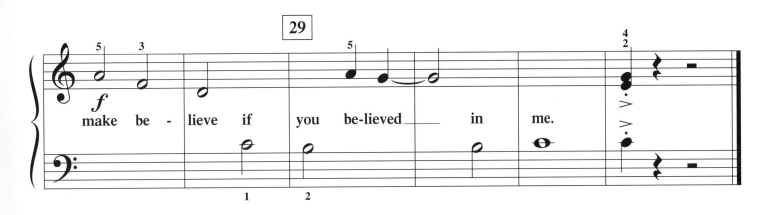

make be - lieve if you be-lieved in me.

f

cresc.

mf

It Don't Mean a Thing If It Ain't Got That Swing

Words and Music by
DUKE ELLINGTON
and **IRVING MILLS**

Teacher Duet: (Student plays 1 octave higher)

Sugarfoot Rag

By NANCY FABER

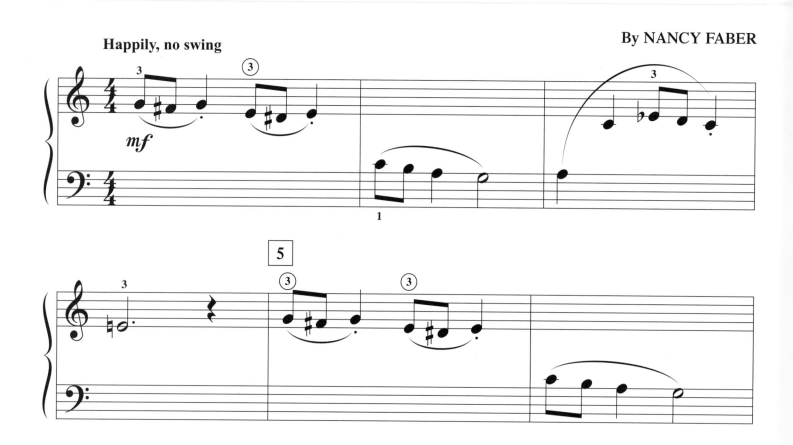

Teacher Duet: (Student plays 2 octaves higher)

From the Paramount Picture BREAKFAST AT TIFFANY'S

Moon River

Words by JOHNNY MERCER

Music by HENRY MANCINI

Moon Riv - er, wid - er than a mile, I'm cross - ing you in style some day. (2 - 3 1 - 2) Old dream - mak - er, you heart - break - er, wher - ev - er you're go - in', I'm go - in' your way. Two

Teacher Duet: (Student plays 1 octave higher)

FF1044

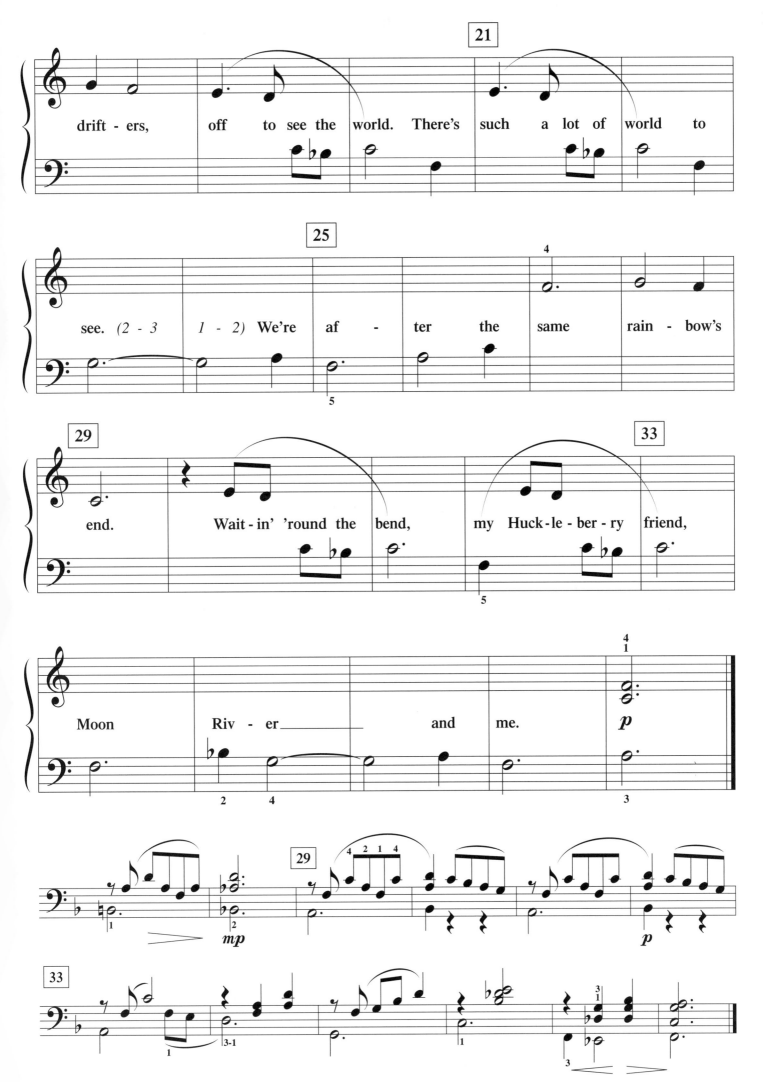

Don't Sit Under the Apple Tree
(With Anyone Else But Me)

Words and Music by
LEW BROWN, SAM H. STEPT
and CHARLIE TOBIAS

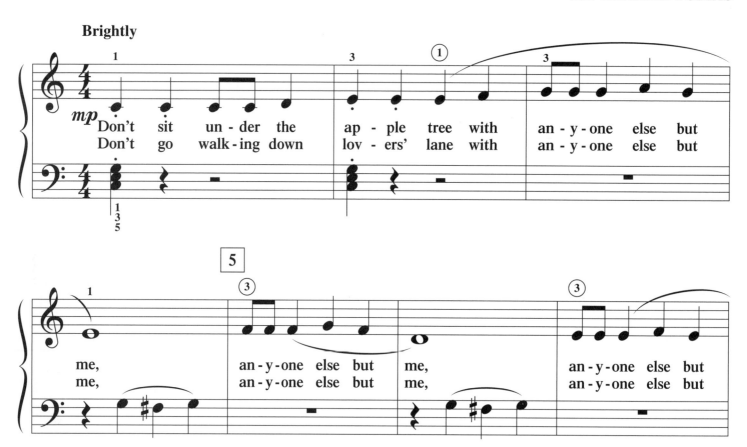

Teacher Duet: (Student plays 1 octave higher)

me. No! No! No!
me. No! No! No!

mf Just re - mem-ber that
Don't sit un - der the

I've been true to
ap - ple tree with

no - bod - y else but
an - y - one else but

you,
me.

f so
You're

just
my

be
L -

true
O -

to
V -

1.

me.

2.

E.

Ain't She Sweet

Happy swing

Words by JACK YELLEN
Music by MILTON AGER

Ain't she sweet? See her com - ing down the
Ain't she nice? Look her o - ver once or

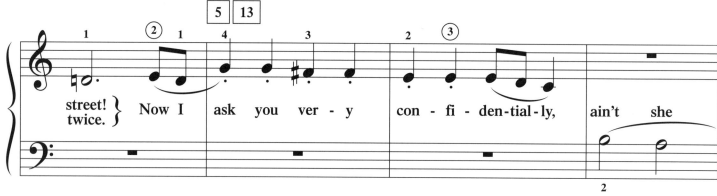

street! twice. Now I ask you ver - y con - fi - den-tial-ly, ain't she

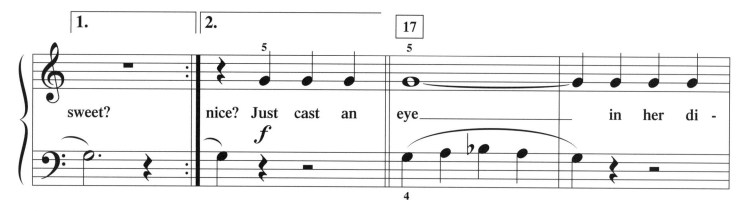

1. sweet?
2. nice? Just cast an eye in her di -

Teacher Duet: (Student plays 1 octave higher)

To Coda

21

FF1044

Boogie-Woogie Fever

Words and Music by
NANCY FABER

Teacher Duet: (Student plays 1 octave higher)

The Blues Monster

Words and Music by
NANCY FABER